SUCCESS SHIFTS

Navigating Your Divine Calling by Faith

Mytecia R. Myles

Special thanks to Marsh V. Cohen for proofreading this work. Special thanks to Dr. Kemi Elufiede for help with editing this work.

Thank you to MyJanae C. Davis and Makiah M. Myles, my two brilliant daughters, for consistent motivation and inspiration. Special thanks to Marsha V. Cohen, my wonderful mother, for being my number one and to Willie (Big Fella) Sims, Jr., my brother, for always reminding me to be amazing and to stop overthinking my next move forward.

Cover design by Davy Mac Promotional (davymacpromtional.com)
Book Interior and E-book Design by Amit Dey | amitdey2528@gmail.com

Printed in the United States of America
First printing edition 2023.
www.supernaturalsuccesspr.net
SuccessShifts@gmail.com

DEDICATION

This book is dedicated to the life and legacy of Bishop Mark Givens, my father, who wholeheartedly lived in Christ without compromise. Your demonstration of living by divine design from the inside and outside has truly left an imprint of illuminating light on my heart.

"Father, the hour has come, Glorify Your Son, that Your Son also may glorify You, as you have given him authority over all flesh, that he should give eternal life to as many as you have given Him. And this is eternal life, that they may know You, the only true God, in Jesus Christ whom You have sent. I have glorified You on the earth. I have finished the work which You have given me to do. And now, O Father, glorify Me together with Yourself, with the glory which I had with You before the world was. "John 17:1-5.

Daddy, may you rest in peace knowing that you have finished the work given to you by God which has given Him the greatest glory and expanded His Kingdom. By looking up to heaven you demonstrated how to align with my Kingdom purpose. The life you lived lifting Christ and seeking things above will be eternally appreciated.

TABLE OF CONTENTS

INTRODUCTION

"...Be fruitful and multiply..." Genesis 2:28

What is the one thing that you desire to accomplish but simply can't seem to accomplish?

What's preventing you from getting it done?

Do you seem to feel stuck or uncertain, but do not have a plan of action on how to proceed forward?

Are you living the life God designed for you?

Are you pursuing peace, love, and joy outside of God?

After years of going through the motions in circles and feeling like a dog chasing its tail, I had concluded that I was actively self-sabotaging my own success and headed for a premature death. What appeared to be external progress and productivity was stressful, uncomfortable, and mentally taxing. I was not fully available to those most important to me and could not effectively produce sustainable growth in my career, business, and socially. Finally, I made a definite decision to get out of my own way and to allow God to do the work within me and around me which was vital to overcoming the internal and external roadblocks. I accepted God's invitation to align with how He saw me and what He declared as my life's purpose. I submitted uncomfortably wholeheartedly to God's promptings.

The decision has allowed the Holy Spirit to give me the truth of what God has planned for me so that I can act on the right things at the right time with the right people and the right environments. I began to ask God a series of questions and even when I did not hear his response I resolved to trust in His process while waiting by faith for an answer. God's refinement of the attitude of my character and of my application and execution of movement interrupted my plans and invited me to get rid of my limited understanding of how he would accelerate and use me for Kingdom advancement. God has a blueprint and through wisdom and understanding, he began to re-establish my heart for a loving rebuild and restoration.

Every day and every moment God will extend an invitation for us to choose Him, His plan, His promises, and His purpose for our lives. God invites us to pursue His master plan concerning our divine calling. This book will help you to get out of your own way, encourage you to identify overthinking roadblocks, and invite you to live a more favorable life with greater confidence and fulfillment. This book is an invitation to you to let go of anything or anyone; therefore, any thoughts and behaviors that have held you back from moving forward and taking intentional action in the pursuit of your Divine calling and Kingdom purpose. As you journey through this book and begin to believe that you play a key role in the momentum of your progress, move from where you are to become engaged in the Holy Spirit as he guides you into your higher calling.

There is no other pursuit in life that will produce successful outcomes, greater peace, joy, and love everlasting. His promises will be fulfilled as you willingly, absolutely with total surrender accept His authority and path. There may be a bit of discomfort in releasing your ideas pertaining to the who, what, how, and when of your life experiences. It is time to lay down and give up self-centered, self-sabotaging, or any desperate pursuit to have it your way, in your own timing without God's plan as your supreme guide. Although we cannot change the past, and neither should we want to, with God's hand and help the trajectory of your life can shift. You can live differently with a great sense of fulfillment.

God knows all about you; you're beginning middle and end, your strengths and weaknesses, your opportunities, and even possible threats. He knows what has been holding you back from moving forward and trusting Him. His process is totally opposite from attempting to position yourself in a place of prestigious power or influence. God's way eliminates the need for a status quo, cultural or environmental approval. As you navigate life and choose to act on God's plan versus your own, keep in mind that He has great plans for you to prosper (3 John 1:2). The Holy Spirit is the one who will guide you, teach you, and transform your thinking and renew your mind for the road ahead. Jesus said, "I have come that they may have life and that they have it more abundantly" (John 10:10). God speaks to you and wants you to be empowered by His Word to understand His ways which are accomplished by faith and following his lead.

It is my desire that your life will be shifted into alignment with what you were born to bring forth. May you persist, be fulfilled, guided, and confirmed by God as a result of going through His processing and using this framework as a tool. May you know the truth of who you are and the authenticity of your unique calling. May you fully awaken and arise to the purposes, promises, and plans of God concerning your very existence so that you will wholeheartedly recognize and accept that your life was strategically designed by The Master Creator. As you navigate through this framework, seek the timing and strategy of God. May you receive everything that God has already established for your success with patience, perseverance, peace, power, and thankful heart?

Let the navigation begin!

CLARITY

"But seek first the kingdom of God and his righteousness, and all these things shall be added to you." Matthew 6:33

Make a Definite Decision

What's holding you back from moving forward in your calling and taking action?

There is significant value in having clarity in decision-making. There are countless benefits of having clarity from peace of mind, eliminating unnecessary actions, demonstrated confidence, and focusing through the execution phase of a project. A success shift occurs at that level of transformation by way of implementation and demonstrates a commitment to acting even before having full knowledge of the details of the pursuit.

Decision-making is the process of making choices by identifying a decision, gathering information, and assessing alternative resolutions. Using a step-by-step decision-making process can help you make more deliberate, thoughtful decisions by organizing relevant information and defining the alternatives (Dartmouth, 2022). Once you realize that you need to decide, begin by clearly knowing the nature of your decision. Why do you need to make a definite decision? Define your situation and discover as much detailed information as possible.

Secondly, seek to establish criteria for a possible solution by gathering relevant and pertinent information. This can be both internal and external searches. Ask God first. He is waiting for your request for His help and insight. This will require patience and consistency. Next, weigh your options and identify if there are untapped possibilities. Are there options that carry a greater value, importance, or priority?

Keep in mind that there will more than likely be more than one possible option. It may be helpful to create a list of possibilities and determine which options line up with God's Word and His instructions to you. Be sure to prioritize your options. Every option will carry its own set of benefits and consequences as well as advantages and disadvantages. Be sure to identify potential distractions as they arise and have a plan for how you will address, ignore or eliminate them.

Next, it's time to act by stepping forward even if you do not have full details. It is not essential to your momentum. Keep going and persevere through the process. Faith without works is dead (James 2:17-26). Do not nullify your definite decision by neglecting to take the next step forward. Guard your mind with God's Word. Remain focused on what He has instructed you to pursue and act without a need for external approval.

Far too often we become distracted by overthinking, mental paralysis, and self-sabotaging behaviors. This can produce stagnation. It decreases momentum and therefore discourages productivity. Lastly, take time to review and evaluate your decision. Are you moving in the right direction and clear regarding your path?

In this final step of the clear decision-making process, keep in mind:

> Clarity allows for persistence in doing something despite difficulty or delay.
>
> Clarity can determine a firm course of action despite opposition or past failures.
>
> Clarity allows personal energy and momentum to generate possibilities.
>
> Clarity provides focus, reflection, and projection.
>
> Clarity opens pathways for transformation and successful outcomes.

We have been given the ability to decide for ourselves and influence the decisions of others. According to Baron

(1988), decisions are made to achieve goals, and they are based on beliefs about what actions will achieve the goals. Decisions carry the weight of small matters and larger life changing matters, such as whether to start a business or pursue an advanced degree. They can be simplistic or complex, involving multiple goals and individuals.

The decision-making process and making a definite decision holds the potential of increased momentum. Once a definite decision has been made it sets into motion a series of events and requires action. If a person decides to start a business, the internal pursuit becomes an external goal that can drive the next thought and following decisions. All movements are the result of thinking.

How we think affects the way we act, believe, set goals, and ultimately live our lives. Our thoughts can hold us back, keep us hostage, and even block us from taking necessary steps toward completing our projects.

According to Byron (1988) in his book on thinking and deciding, there are three basic types of thinking that we must do in order to achieve our goals: thinking about decisions, thinking about beliefs, and thinking about our goals themselves. It also describes what Baron calls the search inference framework, a way of identifying the basic elements in all these thinking processes. Our thinking about our beliefs will be reflective of how we think about ourselves and others. Aligning our thinking with heaven produces unprecedented outcomes. We become more meaningful, our implementation of tactics becomes attainable, and our overall goals become available and attainable. For as a man thinks in his heart, so is he (Proverbs 23:7). Depending on God to help us in our thinking and decision-making making process is key to this success shift. Totally surrendering your mind, your personal will, and your emotions. It will take a mind transformation from thinking at a level of potential to projecting toward possibilities and beginning to meditate on them.

Meditate on these things; give yourself entirely to them that your progress may be evident to all" (1 Timothy 4:15). With clarity of mind, you can begin to implement what you know to be the truth. Success is not a destination. It is a state of being certain or definite. It is built into creation. You have the power to choose. Do not allow things in the past or current circumstances to keep you hostage and prevent you from moving forward into your next destiny step. Awaken to the call of God. Be ready to allow him to move in your life.

Prayer

Heavenly Father, thank you for the new opportunity to seek your promises, plans, and purpose for my career, business, relationships, and other areas of my life. Lord, I know that I have been doubting my gifts and talents and allowing distractions to infiltrate my confidence in making a definite decision. Thank you that I have been forgiven even before

I ask. Father, I desire to know your vision concerning my calling. I want to know your divine plan and to live my life accordingly. I am seeking you before anyone else. What is my path? Whom would you have me meet? Where would you have me live? What should be the primary focus? Lord, help me to make a definite decision and to gain clarity.

I desire to make my next step forward without hesitation or fear that I'm no longer overthinking or blocking my progress. I am asking that you show me what has been holding me back from moving forward or acting. What needs to be removed or added to my daily activities, environment, and plans? I asked for your divine solutions and relevancy. I desire to be persistent and diligent to use the resources that you have already provided. What can I do with what is already in my hands? Father, thank you for clarity, in the mighty name of Jesus I trust you. Amen.

What has God revealed to you?

_____

_____

_____

_____

_____

_____

_____

_____

_____

_____

What action steps can you take today?

_____

_____

_____

_____

_____

_____

_____

_____

_____

Success Shift 2:

COURAGE

"And the LORD, He is the one who goes before you. He will be with you; He will not leave you nor forsake you: do not fear nor be dismayed." Deuteronomy 31:8

Yielded to God

We are given an unlimited number of choices in our lives. We can choose to focus on God's Direction, our own inner fleshly direction, or the direction from some outside voice. In our definite decision to live out our Kingdom purpose, we acknowledge that God is with us and directing us; Therefore, knowing that we are never alone we are given the opportunity to activate courage. With all of life's twists and turns, ascending and descending, God wants us to know that He is forever present and prompting us to choose His ways. God cannot forget about us. He knew us before we were formed in our mother's womb (Jeremiah 1:5).

God knows exactly our every need and every desire, good and not so good. Far too often, people have this idea that they should journey through life solo and sometimes become isolated and withdrawn. We were not created to be alone or navigate our callings outside of God. It is in His best interest that we advance, mature, succeed, prosper, and be in good health in all things (3 John 1:2). Knowing this truth, we can be courageous in our pursuit of fulfilling our divine calling.

The truth is written all throughout God's Word concerning how we are to live and love. In this next success shift, we are invited to accept and believe this truth as we launch forward and take every necessary step towards our goals but courageously yielded to God. This courage found in knowing, believing, and trusting God's Word, propels us over and across man-made boundaries both internal and external. When we yield our plans to the divine plans of God, we stand to do nothing less than succeed. This momentum increases as we seek to do His will so that those around us will see our good works and glorify the Father in heaven (Matthew 5:16). It is never about us. Our yielding and courageous acts are always about others.

It is God in us that does the work (John 14:10). We are to be strong and of good courage, not fearing nor being afraid of any foreseen roadblock. We must be courageous and choose to allow God to lead us forward knowing that He is the only one who goes with us, and the Holy Spirit goes before us.

This knowledge can be our fuel to never ever give up, but to continue forward despite challenges along our paths. will give us strength and fortitude (Deuteronomy 31:6-7).

Personally, I can recall moments when I did not feel courageous at all. I felt depleted, defeated, and as if I had run out of time. After trying to succeed based on cultural and worldly standards, I was left feeling empty and sometimes literally out of breath. After facing multiple health challenges, I realized that my approach was totally out of alignment with the will of God for my life. After making the definite decision to take a different approach and provide God my full and undivided attention my results were no longer self-sabotaging, paralyzing, or potentially life-threatening. No longer did I accept the demands of my employer, family, or social setting as my only option. I submitted to God and watched my peace return. My joy returned. Things that no longer belonged in my environment began to either be removed, resolved or simply disappeared. My confidence had been restored and the great feeling of enthusiasm and eagerness that I had in pursuing God's path was reinstituted and replaced on all levels. I said, "Goodbye, unhealthy living, and HELLO, True Self!"

Although long-suffering can sometimes be rough and strenuous, we have the option to interject patience and fearlessness giving resilience fuel to increase the momentum for a healthy success shift, moving from one place to another, switching the light on, and repositioning our focus.

Courage asks that you allow God to act on your behalf as you accept His rulership and Lordship. As you take your next step forward with courage, you begin to intentionally hear and listen to God. He is repositioning you. Do not look back. Stand firm in your definite decision. What you are about to walk into may appear to be weird or impossible to those around you. The things which are impossible with men are possible with God (Luke 18:27). Obedience is the key that unlocks and fuels the momentum of this success shift. Your next step forward can be dependent on doing and believing what God has instructed you to do even if it frightens you. It would be best to focus on high-impact, on high-impact, high priority, and high value objects and tactics. Ask God to identify your priorities and action steps. Therefore, I say unto you, what things soever ye desire when ye pray, believe that ye receive them, and ye shall have them (Mark 11:24). God wants to change your reality from hopping into believing.

Prayer

Heavenly Father, in the name of Jesus, thank you for being all that I need. As I move forward out of my own way, out of distracting environments and low-energy situations, I ask that You go before me into those spaces that I do not feel qualified or called to. I ask that you forgive me for the times that I have neglected to yield to your help, love, peace, and joy. I am asking that you shift me from entertaining the mindset that keeps me from being bold in my authority in Christ.

Heavenly Father, move me now out of all forms of complacency and mediocrity. Catapult me forward into my next destiny steps. I thank you in advance for your power to persist and persevere regardless of external circumstances. Lord, Jesus, thank you for transforming the way that I think about success. No longer do I yield to status. Father, thank you for courage, in the mighty name of Jesus, I surrender my will to you. Amen.

What has God revealed to you?

_____

_____

_____

_____

_____

_____

_____

_____

_____

What action steps can you take today?

_____

_____

_____

_____

_____

_____

_____

_____

_____

CONFIDENCE

"Now Faith is the substance of things hoped for, and
evidence of things not seen." Hebrews 11:1

Never Doubt God

As you move away from your plan and submit to honoring God as your chief positioning authority, your vision becomes clear. Things that you have never seen before are visible and reachable. Obstacles that had appeared to be immovable now appear mobile and easier to move. God's vision for your lifestyle and legacy becomes clearer; therefore, your confidence in Him experiences a successful shift. This new confidence in God and the things of Him has released you from the prison of dysfunction, disbelief, and inaction. No longer are you paralyzed by doubt or fear of failing.

You have a higher standard of living and know your worth. Your momentum has accelerated.

God gives us divine insight and revelation into our divine calling(s). His Word provides the inspiration, wisdom, and understanding needed to shift from doubt into a state of confidence. Deciding to be rooted in God's understanding and guided by his direction is paramount in this shift. It will allow you to walk, speak, move, engage, and act habitually differently. Andrew Murray in his book Humility: The Journey Toward Holiness, says, "Faith seeks the glory that comes from God, that only comes where God is ALL" (2021). The old way of self-sabotage and doubting will no longer suit your new awareness of purpose.

According to Wilding, M. (2021) impostor syndrome, is a nagging feeling of self-doubt and unworthiness that persists despite obvious achievements. Imposter syndrome is extremely common. Up to 70 percent of professionals say they struggle with it at some point in their careers. In fact, up to 50 percent of men and women face imposter syndrome weekly. "Researchers Pauline Clance and Suzanne Ime's first studied impostor syndrome in the 1970s. It is a psychological phenomenon characterized by the feeling that you are a fake who will be exposed as incapable despite evidence of your intelligence, such as multiple degrees and positive feedback. In other words, impostor syndrome leads you to make inaccurate assessments about your capabilities". According to Wilding (2021):

Common behaviors associated with impostor syndrome include:

Perfectionism - You expect yourself to be the ultimate, all-knowing expert and equate minor mistakes or flaws with failure. Impostor syndrome can lead you to overextend yourself.

Impostor Syndrome - This can lead you to overextend yourself.

Procrastination - You avoid starting or finishing a task because you fear it will prove your inadequacy.

Comparison - You imagine others are smarter and more successful and accomplished than you are.

Overcompensation - You take on more, get more qualifications, and work harder to prove you're good enough.

People Pleasing - You say yes to every request and flex to others' demands to remain likable.

Diminishment - You reject praise and stay out of the spotlight to avoid negative evaluation.

Overcoming Self-Sabotage

In the success shift of confidence, you are given the opportunity to reclaim your authenticity, authority, and peace of mind. No longer are you subjected to the confines of mental paralysis, lower energy, or internal roadblocks. To combat the tendency to procrastinate or neglect to proceed with optimism, instead of stagnation seek first the kingdom of God and his righteousness and these things will be added to you (Matthew 6:33). You do not have to feel paralyzed by the mere thought of pursuing your divine calling. You can pursue that goal with confidence.

Take inventory of self-sabotaging habits and behaviors. Ask the Lord to reveal and uncover his truths concerning your behaviors. Write down God's truth and place them where you can see them daily. Study God's truth. Recite and repeat. Make a conscious effort to activate your faith by living God's truths no matter what reality you are up against. Receive his truth concerning your life, well-being, and future. Review, remember, and walk in freedom. (John 8:32). Distinguish your thoughts and the thoughts of others from the mind of Christ. You do not have to live your life feeling defeated, in comparison to others, diminished, and people-pleasing to be successful in Christ.

God's Word has been designed to encourage, uplift, transform, and cause you to live life more abundantly. The adversary wants you to believe in lies and to rob you of your next destiny step forward in the promises, plans, and purposes for your life. When you experience a thought or imagination that is counteractive to what you know as the truth, decide to turn away from it and resist the desire to believe what is false. Begin to think about things that are true, noble, right, pure, lovely, admirable, excellent, or praiseworthy (Philippians 4:8). Refuse to allow fear of success to hold you in a prison of death. For God hath not given us the spirit of fear; but of power, and of love, and of a sound mind (2 Timothy 1:7).

Do not be ashamed of your calling in God; your Kingdom purpose. Neglect to shrink to fit into spaces or fall into the trap of people-pleasing. Recall your purpose in Christ Jesus daily. Remember that your life has been brought with a price (1 Corinthians 6:20). Therefore, stand firm in who you are as a child of the Most High, God.

Remember that everything and everyone is not meant to be in your ear, providing counsel to your decisions or actions. Begin to take an inventory of your inner circle and environments. Decide what and who must be eliminated. Everything has a season (Ecclesiastes 3:1:1). Every season is not for everyone. Your calling (s) will require you to think, believe, act, and live differently. You are a unique expression of God. Above all else, guard your heart, for everything you do flows from it (Proverbs 4:23). Mastering authenticity over comparison. According to Abdelaal (2020), the comparison is the thief of joy. There will always be someone out there who is smarter, more hardworking, and with more experience than you. While your competitive instinct might set in, it might be more beneficial to learn from your competition instead.

Prayer

Heavenly Father, in the name of Jesus, thank you for your love, your peace, and your joy. Thank you for another opportunity to live life differently, to live life with a sound mind and not be ashamed of the calling that you have placed on my life. Father, thank you for decreeing my life as prosperous and for every season that you have declared it to be fruitful in fulfilling your plans. I embrace every invitation from You and I receive your holy pronouncement of my uniqueness. Father, I thank you for every person and place that I will encounter in your name. I ask that there be an unprecedented positive impact as a result of my confidence in you and your Word. Father, I ask that you shift the trajectory of my thinking in order that I can live life authentically without seeking comparison to man, but only compared to who you have called me to become. Father, shift now, everything in my being. I desire to move forward in holy confidence producing a great harvest and a high return on your investment in my life. Father, thank you for full confidence in You. In the mighty name of Jesus, I surrender my will. Let your will be done. Amen.

What has God revealed to you?

_____

_____

_____

_____

_____

_____

_____

_____

_____

_____

What action steps can you take today?

_____

_____

_____

_____

_____

_____

_____

_____

_____

COMMUNICATION

"Let no corrupt word proceed out of your mouth,
but what is good for necessary edification, that it may
impart grace to the hearers." Ephesian 4:29

Conscious Engagement

You will know that a supernatural success shift has occurred when your heart has been redirected and fully immersed into the business of God, towards Him, and totally dependent on Jesus. Anything else is secondary or minute. Your focus will be strategically placed on the things that seek to understand people and how to organize impact. It will require authentic connections, collaboration, and community-building tactics. But, without God's direction, this shift may feel like a burdensome act of tolerance.

Your resilience will be tested. Be mindful of your methods and movements. Learn the four different factors of communication: speaking, reading, listening, and writing. In the successful shift of communication, your character, conduct, and compassion will all be refined. "Whether you choose to communicate better with your husband, kids, co-workers or employers, learning may help you make stronger relationships, develop greater trust, respect, problem-solving, improve collaboration, and your complete social and emotional health" (A. A. Adu-Oppong and E. Agyin-Birikorang, 2014). Each factor of this success shift can help you to build quality over quantity networks.

Healthy relationships are key to personal and professional development. As you navigate your divine calling by faith, your communication with others both verbal and nonverbal will be paramount to your success. "Communication is one of the most important components of our lives. It influences how people connect in both their personal and professional lives. Good communication is the foundation for building respect and trust" (Sumaiya, B., Srivastava, S, 2022).

Self-Control

What happens in our lives when we take on counter-productive behaviors such as overthinking and allow an uncontrolled state of mental paralysis to block us from making definite decisions, moving forward in the pursuit of progress, or accomplishing unfinished goals? The uncontrollable stress that is set off unconsciously has the potential to weaken our health and well-being as well as consume and rob us of valuable time.

Surrendering our lives fully withholding nothing to God including our thoughts and societal programming can give us freedom and capacity to create an action strategy that has the potential of delivering healthier more predictable behaviors. We have all heard how stress can kill. After you have made a definite decision and gained clarity of mind it is important that we have an action plan for our next steps forward. Having a plan and being intentional to use it as a meter or indicator of our proximity to our goal can be extremely helpful. Without a plan, we invite unwanted and unnecessary stress, physically, mentally, emotionally, economically, relationally, and financially. "The new research demonstrates that acute, uncontrollable stress sets off a series of chemical events that weaken the influence of the prefrontal cortex while strengthening the dominance of older parts of the brain" (Arnsten A, Mazure CM, Sinha R., 2012).

Top 10 Obstacles to Navigating Your Divine Calling by Faith

Distrusting God

Skepticism

Lack of Self-Control

Worry

Doubt

Fear

Mental Paralysis

External Distractions

Lack of Discipline

Unambitious

Unmotivated

Pride of life

What has God spoken to you about these obstacles?

Before taking your next step forward, pause to take an inventory and analyze your strengths, areas of improvement, and opportunities. Decide to write down your wins, accomplishments, and successes. Be mindful that you have come a long way and have overcome multiple obstacles. Don't be so hard on yourself as you work through the inventory.

My Strengths

_____

_____

_____

_____

_____

_____

_____

_____

_____

_____

Stressful Behaviors

_____

_____

_____

_____

_____

_____

_____

_____

_____

Opportunities for Growth

Are you knowingly or unknowingly sabotaging your next success shift? Take this Inventory.

1. I second-guess God's Word.
2. I had a difficult time completing tasks, and projects, or reaching my goals.
3. I overthink my decisions and talk myself out of taking a step forward.
4. I doubt my ability to succeed because of my past.
5. I typically wait for confirmation from external sources before trusting God.
6. I find it difficult to accept my uniqueness in God.
7. I rarely ask for help because I do not want to appear incompetent.
8. I worry about what other people will think about my success.
9. I think my family will not want to be around me if I pursue my calling.
10. I have given permission for doubt to penetrate my thoughts about growth and prosperity.

If you answered yes to three or more of these questions, this may be an indicator that you are not clear in who you are, your divine calling, or actively preventing your productivity and growth.

Are you willing to identify obstacles and self-sabotaging behavior?

_____

_____

_____

_____

_____

_____

_____

_____

_____

What is holding you back from moving forward and acting?

_____

_____

_____

_____

_____

_____

_____

_____

_____

What are your strategies and steps that you can take today, within the next three days, 14 days, or 30 days? Begin to create your strategy by revisiting God's Vision for you. Next, set measurable goals personally and professionally. Then, create at least three objects based on your goals. Lastly, identify action steps that you plan to take.

_____

_____

_____

_____

_____

_____

Today, I am willing to take these action steps towards moving forward:

_____

_____

_____

_____

_____

_____

_____

Within the next three days, I am willing to take these action steps towards moving forward:

_____

_____

_____

_____

_____

_____

_____

_____

Within the next 14 days, I am willing to take these action steps towards moving forward:

_____

_____

_____

_____

_____

_____

_____

_____

_____

Within the next 30 days, I am willing to take these action steps towards moving forward:

_____

_____

_____

_____

_____

_____

_____

_____

_____

_____

_____

_____

_____

_____

_____

_____

_____

CULTIVATION

But the fruit of the spirit is love, joy, peace, longsuffering,
kindness, goodness, faithfulness, gentleness, and
self-control. against such things, there is no law."
Galatians 5:22-23

Maximum Consistency

We have been designed to reach peak performance. The standards, ethics, and integrity of culture and social economic environments can sometimes diminish our vision. Therefore, we must set targeted boundaries and strategies to help us focus on the calling of God. In addition, there must be sensitivity, maturity, and the pursuit of excellence that helps in discerning potential distractions and opportunities. Remembering to remember, it's all about God, His divine plan.

In this fifth success shift of cultivation, you're invited to elevate your skills by being more intentional in prioritization. The key is to nurture, build up, and uproot on a regular continuous ongoing basis. It will be necessary to take inventory and assess how your goals, objectives, and actions align with God's plan for your life. Create a plan of action based on your findings. Seek additional help when necessary. God has a timeline for all things concerning your divine calling. It is your choice to be consistent in cultivating, aligning, and shifting with God. There is an evidential difference between when you are in alignment and when you are not. It's time to allow God to straighten every crooked area and soar.

Prayer

Heavenly Father, in the name of Jesus, Thank you for another successful shift. Thank you for allowing me to finish this process. Father, your Word says to be fruitful and to multiply. I asked you to open my eyes and understand in order that I can maximize cultivation and consistency and navigate my divine calling. continue to show me where I am out of line and potentially holding myself back from moving forward. Father, I asked you to increase the momentum now in order that you will be glorified by the fruit. Let there be a great harvest that manifests and most importantly show me Guide Me and teach me your Divine will. Father, thank you for maximum consistency in due season, in the mighty name of Jesus, I transcend far above every roadblock to fulfilling your purpose. Amen.

What has God revealed to you?

_____

_____

_____

_____

_____

_____

_____

_____

What action steps can you take today?

_____

_____

_____

_____

_____

_____

_____

_____

_____

_____

CONCLUSION

The ultimate success in life is to know God, His will, your Kingdom purpose, and to live your divine calling by faith under His guidance. Our daily activities, in our homes, through our careers, in our business endeavors, and in other life pursuits. If we have the audacity and the willingness to take bold risks, knowing that we have been prepared and positioned properly to be used by God; then there is nothing more confirming than having clarity of thought, courage, confidence, and the ability to effectively communicate.

The five success shifts that have been presented within this book are only a small portion of what is available to those who seek God, His Kingdom, and His authority before making decisions in life. We have been given unique gifts, skills, talents, opportunities, and favor that are to be used to fulfill our greatest achievements in God. Let it be resolved that self-sabotage, distractions, overthinking, and sluggish momentum seize today. Pursue God no matter what you are facing in life. Let your light shine! Manifest the will of God.

REFERENCES

Adu-Oppong, A. A., & Agyin-Birikorang, E. (2014) [Online]. Communication in the workplace: Guidelines for improving effectiveness. Glob. J. Commer. Manag. Perspect, 3(5), 1-6. Retrieved from https://www.longdom.org/articles/communication-in-the-workplace-guidelines-for-improving-effectiveness.pdf

Arnsten A, Mazure CM, Sinha R. (2012). This is your brain in meltdown. Sci Am. Apr;306(4):48-53. doi: 10.1038/scientificamerican0412-48. PMID: 22486116; PMCID: PMC4774859.

Baron, J. (1988). Thinking and deciding. Cambridge, UK: Cambridge University Press.

Graham, B. (2006). The Journey: How to Live by Faith in An Uncertain World. W Publishing Group.

University of Massachusetts, Dartmouth (2022). Decision-making process. https://www.umassd.edu/fycm/decision-making/process/

Abdelaal, G. (2020). Coping with imposter syndrome in academia and research. Biochem (Lond); 42 (3): 62–64. doi: https://doi.org/10.1042/BIO20200033

Murray, A. (2021). Humility: The Journey Toward Holiness. CreateSpace Publishing. pg. 42.

Petrocelli, J. V., Tormala, Z. L., & Rucker, D. D. (2007). Unpacking attitude certainty: Attitude clarity and attitude correctness. Journal of Personality and Social Psychology, 92(1), 30–41. https://doi.org/10.1037/0022-3514.92.1.30

Bushra Sumaiya, Subododh Srivastava, Vipin Jain, and Ved Prakash (2022). The Role of Effective Communication Skills in Professional Life. World Journal of English Language, Vol 12, No 2. Academia.edu. https://doi.org/10.5430/wjel.v12n3p134

Wilding M. (2021). Tame self-sabotage and cultivate self-confidence. Talent Development. 75(9):78-80. https://libezproxy.syr.edu/login?url=https://www.proquest.com/trade-journals/tame-self-sabotage-cultivate-confidence/docview/2570254159/se-2.

ABOUT THE AUTHOR

A native of Detroit, MI, Mytecia Myles is a creative, bold, and innovative leader. She is the founder and Global Head of PR and Communications of Supernatural Success, LLC., a PR & communications consulting firm specializing in the literary, travel, and luxury hospitality sectors. Myles is a business advisor, international speaker, editor, and small business mentor. She is a contributing writer for the International Luxury Hotelier Magazine. She consults brands and organizations on how to influence success in their sphere of influence.

Myles is a brainchild of the Nashville Freedom of Voice, Youth Writer's Workshop 2019 Literary Project which was in collaboration with the Leaders Are Readers Program (LARP), the Porch Nashville, Nashville Public Library, Metro Nashville Arts Commission, Education Equal Opportunity Group (EEOG), Nashville Museum of African

American Music, and Ingram Content Group. Myles has had the honor of working with a diverse group of writers and young aspiring writers in helping them in becoming published authors. She is the creator of He Who Has An Ear, Kingdom Writer's Workshop where she helps aspiring authors map and birth their stories into print or other multimedia content. Myles serves as a PR writer for non-profits where she provides strategic communications, content coordination, and social media insights. Myles is a licensed minister at First Baptist Church Murfreesboro (TN) and the mother of two brilliant adult daughters.

Printed in the USA
CPSIA information can be obtained
at www.ICGtesting.com
LVHW040540080224
771186LV00059B/1605